This workbook belongs to: _____

food smarts
Adult Workbook

ISBN: 978-1726294751

Some vector art included was provided by Vecteezy.com and freepik.com.
Printed by CreateSpace in the United States of America.

v.08272018

Contents

■ Getting Started 5

    Exploring Our Food History 6

    Feeding Our Families 7

    Cooking with EatFresh.org 8

    Your Nutrition Goals 9

    Goal Tracker 11

    Decoding Food Labels 12

    The Plant-Focused Diet 14

    Food Journal 15

■ Feeding Your Family 17

    Feeding Baby, Feeding Mom 18

    Welcome to the Table! 19

    Positive Feeding: Toddlers and Preschoolers 20

    Positive Feeding: Elementary and Middle School Kids 21

    Kids in the Kitchen 22

■ Cooking 23

    Kitchen Safety Review 24

    Healthier Cooking with Limited Space and Money 25

    Cooking for One 26

    Saving Time When Cooking 27

    Small Appliances for Small Spaces 28

    Glossary of Recipe Terms 29

    How to Read a Recipe 30

■ Creating a Balanced Meal 31

    My Plate 32

    My Healthy Eating Plate 33

    Food Group Bingo 34

    My Family's Rainbow of Fruits and Vegetables 35

    Eat the Rainbow! 36

    Know Your Serving Sizes 37

    Portion Size Hand Comparison 38

■ Choosing Whole Foods 39

    Grocery Store Heroes 40

    Choosing and Using Healthy Fats 41

Eating Out and Staying Healthy..42

Eating Foods In-Season 43

Make Half Your Grains Whole 44

Rethink Your Drink 45

Make These Meals Healthier 47

Go, Slow, STOP! 48

Grain Game..49

Bean Game 50

Don't Call Me Sugar!..51

The Leah's Pantry DO EAT Food List..52

Healthy Swaps 54

Being a Smart Consumer..55

Food Labels—Nutrition Facts...56

Food Labels—Ingredients Lists 58

Food Label Scavenger Hunt...60

Anatomy of a Grocery Store 61

Nutrition Labels Comparison..62

Outsmarting the Grocery Store 64

Food Advertisements 65

Creating a Meal Plan & Grocery List..66

Meal Plan & Grocery List Follow-Up 68

Seafood and Mercury...69

Farmers' Markets..70

Do You Qualify for a Nutrition Assistance Program? 71

Shelf-Stable Food Extensions..72

Tips to Store Your Produce to Make it Last Longer.....................................74

Stay Healthy 77

Fuel Your Brain...78

Make Moving Fun! 79

Healthy Changes 80

Sleep Your Way to Health...81

Diabetes: Know the Risk 82

Sodium and Healthy Blood Pressure 83

Strong Bones for Life..84

GETTING STARTED

Exploring Our Food History

■ **Consider these questions on your own or in a group.**

1. Which foods do you associate with your childhood?
   -Are these foods everyday meals or meals served on special occasions?
   -Do you make any of these meals for yourself now?

2. Who taught you about cooking, diet, and nutrition? Who have you taught about cooking, diet, and nutrition?

3. What are your comfort foods? What foods do you crave when you are tired, cold, or sick?

4. What are your favorite foods to eat?

5. What are some reasons people eat?

6. Why do you eat? Have these reasons changed over the course of your lifetime?

7. Do you know where your food comes from?

8. Do you trust grocery stores, restaurants, and advertisements with regard to the information they give you about food?

9. What information would you like to learn from this class?

▌Do you provide meals for your family?

Discuss these questions in pairs or groups.

1. What are the most challenging aspects of feeding your family healthy meals?

2. What are the biggest concerns about your children's eating habits?

3. What are your mealtime rituals?

4. What prevents your family from eating together?

5. Does your family plan meals out in advance? Who does the planning?

6. How frequently do you eat take-out or fast food? Home-cooked meals?

7. Do you prohibit your children from eating certain foods?

8. How do you encourage your children to eat?

9. Do certain foods give you more energy?

10. What foods are your "comfort foods"?

Cooking with EatFresh.org

■ Where do you find trustworthy nutrition information online?

EatFresh.org makes shopping and home cooking easy. Go to EatFresh.org right now and start exploring!

» Find healthy, inexpensive, and quick recipes.

» Print, save, share, and text recipes to your mobile phone.

» Learn lifestyle tips to keep you healthy and feeling your best.

» Ask a question to the EatFresh.org dietitian.

» Save time planning and shopping with meal plans.

» Apply for CalFresh/SNAP.

» Learn basic cooking skills and how to substitute ingredients to use what you already have at home.

» View the website in English, Spanish, or Chinese.

» View nutrition information for each recipe.

Have you ever set a health goal and achieved it? How?

Try this approach: *Dream Big*

First, sit quietly for a moment with your eyes closed. Imagine yourself one year from now, living a healthier life. Let yourself dream big even if you don't know how to achieve your dream! How is your dream life different from your life now? Where are you? Who are you with? What words or pictures come to mind? Make notes here.

[content continues on next page...]

Then: *Start Small*

Now try to think of one small goal for this week to move towards your dream.
Your goal should be SMART:

» **Specific**—Avoid words like "more," "less" or "better."

» **Measurable**—Will you know when you've achieved it?

» **Action Based**—Not everything is in your control; choose goals that relate to your actions.

» **Realistic**—Choose goals you're likely to accomplish. Start small.

» **Time Frame**—Set a goal to achieve this week.

Some examples

» I will switch from white rice to brown rice twice this week.

» I will eat a piece of fruit with my breakfast every morning this week.

» I will cook a hot dinner three times this week.

» I will try two new foods this week.

How could the following goals be improved?

1. I will lose weight.

2. I will eat less saturated fat and more fiber.

3. I will never eat fast food again.

TRY IT! Fill in the blanks to create two SMART Goals you might set for the coming week. Then choose one to track using the following page.

I will _____ _____ this week.
(action)   (how often)

I will _____ _____ this week.
(action)   (how often)

Goal Tracker

◼ What keeps you motivated?

Choose a SMART goal from page 10 to work on for a few weeks. Then, each week, reflect on your goal and your progress.

I will _____ _____ this week.

                   (action)   (how often)

To gauge your progress, ask yourself:

» Did I achieve my goal this past week? Why or why not?

» What was challenging about my goal?

» What was easy?

» Should I continue working on this goal or create a new one? If so, what is it?

Week (end of)	My Progress
1	
2	
3	
4	
5	
6	

Decoding Food Labels

What words do you look for on food labels?

Whole foods like fresh vegetables often have no labels. But labels on canned, boxed, or bagged foods can be confusing. Check out these common label terms.

Fat is needed in small amounts to help the body absorb some vitamins. **Saturated fat** is one type. It comes mostly from animal products. **Trans fat** is another type. It is found in processed foods, but should be avoided.

Carbohydrates provide energy. **Sugars** are one type that provide quick energy. **Starches** are another type. These must be broken down through digestion. **Fiber** cannot be broken down for energy. It carries water and other waste through the body.

Proteins are the building blocks of cells, muscles, and tissues. Most whole foods besides fruits have some protein.

Vitamins are compounds needed by the body in various amounts.

Minerals like sodium, potassium, and magnesium occur in nature.

» **Enriched** foods have had nutrients replaced after food processing. Enriched flour, for example, has had B vitamins added to replace those lost in processing. Keep in mind: Enriched foods are not always healthier. This label is usually found on foods that are processed. Natural whole foods have not had anything removed in the first place!

» **Free range** meat, eggs, and dairy generally come from animals given access to the outdoors. The USDA regulates this label only for chicken. California requires it for eggs.

» **Fortified** foods have had nutrients added. Orange juice may be fortified with calcium, for example, since people who drink it may be at risk for low calcium.

» **Gluten-free** foods have no gluten, a protein found in some grains (wheat, kamut, spelt, barley, rye, and sometimes oats).

Keep in mind: Some people avoid gluten due to a condition called celiac disease. Others simply feel better when they don't eat it. The use of this label is not USDA regulated.

» **Low-sodium** foods contain less than 140 mg of sodium per serving. This label is regulated by the FDA. Keep in mind: The phrase "low-sodium" is also used casually about items with less sodium than usual. On a label however, it means the item has less than 140 mg per serving.

» **Non-GMO** foods are produced without genetically modified organisms. Keep in mind: Many people choose non-GMO foods out of concern for possible unknown effects of GMOs on the Earth and human health.

» **No salt/unsalted** foods are free of added salt. They may still have natural sodium.

[content continues on next page...]

» **Organic** food is made or grown without most chemicals, human waste, or GMOs. Organic meats come from animals not given antibiotics or growth hormones. Keep in mind: Some people choose organic foods to avoid chemicals. Others like that organic farming is gentler on the Earth. Note that many farmers use organic practices but cannot afford to be officially certified "organic." The use of this label is USDA regulated.

» **Pastured** applies to animals who roam freely and eat what they would in nature.

» **rBST-free** dairy comes from cows that have not been given rBST growth hormone. This hormone is used to make cows produce more milk. Keep in mind: Studies have shown rBST harms cows and may be linked to cancer in humans.

» **Sugar-free** foods must contain less than .5 grams of sugar per serving and no added sugars. Keep in mind: Sugar-free does not mean no carbohydrates! Also note, the small amount of sugar in these foods adds up if you eat many servings. This label is regulated by the FDA.

» **Vegan** foods are free of all animal products. This label is not well-regulated.

» **Whole grain** foods contain grains (such as whole wheat) with all 3 edible parts intact: the bran, endosperm and germ. Keep in mind: Look for foods labeled 100% whole grain or that have whole grains as a first ingredient.

■ Smart Choices for Canned, Boxed, and Bagged Foods:

» Choose foods made from ingredients that you can picture in their raw state or growing in nature. If you see something you can't pronounce and think was made in a lab, look out.

» Don't be fooled by big health claims on a package. Health claims such as "low-fat" can distract you from something less healthy such as high sugar or sodium.

» Avoid foods with sugar listed in the first three ingredients. Look out for hidden added sugars.

» Look for 100% whole grain foods; find this label or the word "whole" in the first ingredient (whole oats, whole wheat, whole corn).

The Plant-Focused Diet

▌ Why eat plants?

The United States Department of Agriculture (USDA) advises eating lots of plant foods each day. It also gives tips for people who follow a vegetarian eating pattern. Most vegetarians skip meats in favor of plant proteins like tofu and legumes. Some avoid dairy and eggs too.

Some benefits of eating mostly plants

» many whole plant foods are rich in fiber

» whole plant foods are low in sodium

» whole plant foods are high in vitamins and minerals

» plant foods have less saturated fat than animal foods and no cholesterol

» many plant proteins, like beans, are cheap and easy to prepare

One study from the 2017 Journal of the American College of Cardiology showed that people who ate mostly plants had a lower risk for heart disease than people who didn't—but only if they ate mostly whole, natural plant foods. In other words, according to the Harvard School of Public Health, "reducing animal foods doesn't necessarily lead to greater heart protection if the resulting diet is based on less healthy plant foods."

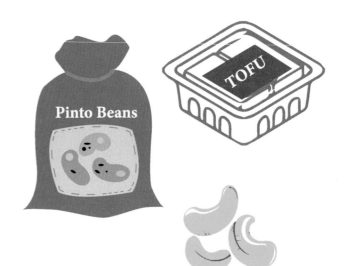

▌ If you want to cut back on animal foods...

1. Enjoy plant protein sources like nuts, seeds, legumes and soy foods like tofu and tempeh.

2. Get vitamin B12 from dairy or fortified cereals.

3. Enjoy calcium-rich plant foods like fortified soy milk and dark leafy greens if you also do not eat dairy.

4. Choose whole foods over processed foods. Whole grains, vegetables, and legumes have enough protein to meet most people's needs; junk foods made from white flour and sugar do not!

▌ Ideas

» For breakfast, try a cooked whole grain like oatmeal or quinoa with fruit.

» For lunch, try a black bean burger on whole grain bread. Or enjoy a vegetable salad with beans, nuts, or seeds on top.

» For dinner, make a one-pot meal like a lentil soup or chili. Or, stir-fry vegetables with tofu, and serve over brown rice.

 **TRY IT!** How can you create a SMART Goal around adding more whole plant foods to your diet?

Food Journal

■ Are you aware of what you are eating?

Keep a food journal for three days. Include specifics about amounts and ingredients.

DAY			
Breakfast			
Lunch			
Dinner			
Snacks			

FEEDING YOUR FAMILY

■ What is hard about feeding your infant? What about feeding yourself?

Breastfeeding Tips

1. Learning to breastfeed may take time and effort. This is normal!

2. Switch breasts about halfway through each feeding, or from one feeding to the next.

3. Flavors and compounds from foods you eat can end up in breast milk. Spicy or gassy foods, like cabbage, may cause problems for your baby.

4. Check with your doctor to see if alcohol or medications are safe for you while breastfeeding.

5. Your baby should dirty several diapers per day. This is one sign he or she is eating enough.

■ Mom Needs Care, Too

It can be tough to take care of yourself while taking care of someone else! Remember:

1. Avoid restricting calories if breastfeeding in the first 6 months.

2. An eating pattern of mostly whole foods may help you recover from pregnancy and delivery faster.

3. Keep healthy, ready-to-eat foods on hand for when cooking is impossible. Fresh fruit, cut vegetables, yogurt, nuts, and whole grain bread are good choices.

4. Drink extra water through the day if you are breastfeeding.

5. Limit alcohol, caffeine, and added sugars. These can disrupt your sleep cycle. It's hard enough to sleep with a newborn around!

■ Infants...

» should be breast-fed every three hours (more if needed) or given a bottle of formula as directed by your doctor.

» vary in how long they nurse at one time. Some need as few as 10 minutes, others as much as 60 minutes.

» should get most of their nutrition from breast milk, or formula, only until 6 months old.

Welcome to the Table!

Is your baby ready for solid foods?

Your baby may be ready if he or she:

» holds up its head by itself

» sits up with help

» shows interest in the food you are eating

» accepts spoon-fed food without tongue thrusting

Babies should get their nutrition from breast milk or formula for the first 6 months. After that, they can begin to try soft, mild foods. You can prepare your own with a blender, food processor, or food mill. Iron-fortified cereal, oatmeal, banana, avocado, and sweet potato are great first choices (mix with water, breast milk, or formula only). Eggs, yogurt, well-cooked chicken, mashed fish, and other pureed vegetables can be added soon after. Finger foods like Cheerios, firm tofu, grated cheese, or banana cubes can be given around 7 months under close supervision. Nut and peanut products can be included as long as they are not a choking hazard.

Tips

1. Add new foods every 4-5 days. Watch for any food allergies.

2. Change the food from smooth to chunky as your child grows.

3. Do not chew food yourself before giving it to your child.

4. Spoon feed at the beginning of a meal; finger foods at the end.

5. Encourage drinking from an open cup, sippy cup, or straw cup.

6. Whole fruit is better than juice. If you do serve juice, offer no more than 4 oz. per day of 100% fruit juice, diluted with water, in a cup not a bottle.

7. Avoid honey until after 12 months.

8. Never leave a baby alone with food!

Make Your Own!

Some ideas:

» Put brown rice or oatmeal in a blender for 2 full minutes. Add to water in a saucepan and simmer for 10 minutes. Whisk or stir to avoid lumps.

» Wash and peel apples or pears. Cut into pieces and simmer with water until soft. Puree.

» Store homemade baby food in the fridge for 3 days. For longer storage, freeze in ice cube trays, then transfer to a plastic bag.

TRY IT! Which of the ideas above would you like to try? What other strategies do you know?

What are the challenges to feeding your young child?

Toddlers...

» are growing teeth, but are still at high risk for choking.

» may change tastes and appetite from day to day.

» may prefer foods in their simplest form (without sauce or mixed with other foods).

» like to "play" with food using all their senses; plan for this rather than discouraging it.

Preschoolers...

» may need to be exposed to new foods many times before acceptance.

» are ready for more structured mealtimes and food routines.

» are more exposed to processed foods outside the home but can begin to learn about healthy decision-making.

Young children learn by imitation. Enjoy eating fruits, veggies, and whole grains, and eventually your kids will, too!

What to Offer?

» 16-24 oz whole milk per day for kids 12-24 months. Switch to low-fat at 24 months.

» After age 1, tummies can handle berries, tomatoes, citrus, and honey.

» Three meals plus two healthy snacks per day at predictable times.

» Mild versions of whatever the rest of the family is eating. It's not necessary to cook a separate menu.

Picky Eating?

» Your child might become more "picky" as he or she gets older. This is normal!

» Be patient as your child tries new foods. He or she may need to try something several times before accepting it. Patience works better than pressure.

» Never force a child to eat. Young kids eat different amounts every day.

» Young kids love to dip! They may be more willing to try new foods they can dip it in yogurt, hummus, nut butter, or salsa.

Make Time for Mealtime

» Cook together, eat together, talk together. Turn off the TV and cell phones. Make mealtime family time!

» Involve kids in the process of preparing meals and cleaning up.

Remember: You decide **what** *and* **when** *to eat, kids decide* **how much.**

© Copyright 2006-2018 Leah's Pantry Food Smarts Workshop • *See Instructor Binder for companion info.*

What are the challenges to feeding your growing child?

Elementary School Kids...

» are beginning to understand where food comes from and that some foods are good for growing bodies.

» need to be active every day for physical and mental health.

» want to do things their peers are doing.

» may feel guilty about eating animals.

» benefit from structured mealtimes as they develop decision-making skills.

Adolescents...

» need to be active every day for physical and mental health.

» may start to see connections between diet, physical appearance, and health.

» may be more adventurous with food choices.

» are vulnerable to peer pressure around what to eat and how to look.

» may gain weight more rapidly with the onset of adult hormones.

Make Fruits and Vegetables Fun

» Keep a bowl of fresh fruit on the kitchen table.

» Put washed and cut fruits and veggies on a shelf in your refrigerator where your child can see them.

» Let them pick fruits and veggies at the store.

» Experiment with dips and spice powders to make these foods more interactive.

Hungry Kid Tip—Kids are usually hungry right when they get home from school or right before you begin making dinner. Having sliced fruits and veggies already prepared makes it easy to feed them.

Kids in the Kitchen

▣ How can kids help with food preparation?

Kids gain life skills by learning to cook. They are also more likely to try foods they help make. Giving kids jobs can help them feel important and grown-up, too.

Safety for Kids of All Ages

» Always wash hands before cooking. Use soap and warm water, and sing the ABCs.

» Do not eat foods with raw egg.

» Have kids stand at the level of activity. Use a chair if necessary.

» Keep knives out of reach of small children.

» Put kid-safe plastic bowls, plates, and cups where kids can reach them.

» Choose kid-friendly recipes to cook together. Consult the Leah's Pantry recipe book or EatFresh.org for ideas!

Toddlers are learning to use their arms and hands. They can...

» scrub veggies and fruit; wash and tear greens.

» help choose foods at the grocery store.

» carry unbreakable items to the table.

» be very messy... cook before bath time!

Three- to five-year-olds are learning to use their fingers. They can...

» measure ingredients, with help.

» mix wet or dry ingredients.

» spread peanut butter, cream cheese, or hummus.

» knead, roll out dough, and cut dough with cookie cutters.

» set, clear, and wipe the table.

» peel some fruits and veggies as well as hard-boiled eggs.

» mash soft fruits and veggies or cut with a plastic or butter knife.

» juice oranges, lemons, and limes.

Kids ages 6 and up can follow multi-step directions and experiment. They can...

» begin to practice with "real" knives; always supervise!

» make salads including salad dressing.

» measure and follow increasingly complex recipes.

» help with simple stove top recipes: stirring scrambled eggs, flipping grilled cheese or pancakes (always supervise).

» begin to experiment based on personal taste.

» find connections between cooking and science/math concepts.

 **Which jobs could your child help with? Which would he or she like most?**

COOKING

Kitchen Safety Review

▌ Why is it important to practice good food safety?

Follow these tips to create a safer kitchen.

1. Keep food preparation surfaces (cutting boards, counters, etc.) clean, since these are breeding grounds for bacteria.

   » If you use a cutting board and knife to cut raw meat, fish or poultry, be sure to clean and sanitize the surface before using it again. Some people keep two cutting boards: one for raw foods and one for ready-to-eat foods.

2. Cook foods thoroughly.

   » When meat is exposed to air, bacteria immediately begins to develop. For that reason, hamburgers must always be cooked through, while a steak is safe to eat medium rare.

   » To be safe, invest in a meat thermometer and test the meat for doneness.

3. Store raw meat and uncooked food on a lower shelf of your refrigerator.

   » Also, keep eggs off the door and near the back where temperatures remain the coldest.

   » Your refrigerator should be kept at 40° F or less.

4. Refrigerate prepared foods within two hours of cooking or buying them.

   » Properly refrigerated food can be eaten for 3-5 days. When in doubt, throw it out!

5. There are four ways to safely defrost foods:

   » Overnight in the refrigerator.

   » In a bowl of cold water, with the water changed every 30 minutes.

   » In the microwave.

   » During cooking.

   Note: It is NEVER safe to leave frozen meat out on the counter top to defrost.

6. To ensure you have clean hands, wash them in hot, soapy water for at least 20 seconds. When teaching kids, have them sing the ABCs while washing.

7. When you wash dishes, either use an automatic dishwasher or wash them in the sink and allow to air dry.

   » Damp dish towels can harbor bacteria.

Healthier Cooking with Limited Space and Money

What are the challenges to cooking when you don't have much space or money? What are some other solutions?

CHALLENGE There's not much space for produce in my small fridge.

SOLUTION Only store items in the fridge/freezer that need to be in there. Some fruits and veggies can stay out. See page 63.

CHALLENGE Healthy food can sometimes seem to be the most expensive.

SOLUTION Staying healthy can decrease a person's costs in the long term, so it's important to eat healthy as often as possible.

- » Look for coupons.
- » Only spend money on healthy food. Unhealthy food may be cheap, but it provides no nutrition.
- » Meat is expensive. Try eating vegetarian a few times a week.
- » Buy foods in bulk. If storage is a problem, ask a friend to split the food and the bill.
- » Scour the neighborhood: do you know where free, healthy meals are being served?
- » Use the food from the food bank! It's free and there is often a lot of fresh produce.
- » Avoid corner stores and seek out the closest grocery store with the best deals.

CHALLENGE I only have a microwave.

SOLUTION Check with your building management to see if you can invest in a rice cooker, slow cooker (crock-pot), or toaster oven. Also, microwaves aren't just for reheating. They can be used to cook fresh meals from scrambled eggs to pasta. Check EatFresh.org for ideas! Thrift stores like Goodwill are great places to find very inexpensive kitchen items.

CHALLENGE There are no grocery stores close by and the small stores near me don't sell much produce.

SOLUTION Read ingredient lists and nutrition facts labels to find the healthiest food at corner stores.

- » Avoid foods with sugar as the first ingredient, partially hydrogenated oil (trans fat), and more than 140 mg sodium per serving.
- » Choose whole wheat or whole grain products. Whole wheat or another whole grain should be the first listed in the ingredient list.
- » The fewer the ingredients listed, the better.
- » Some examples: vegetable soup over meat soup, plain potato chips, pretzels or popcorn instead of flavored chips or other bagged snacks, whole grain cereals, breads and crackers, water or milk instead of soft drinks.
- » Sometimes drug stores like Walgreens or CVS have very good deals on canned tuna, canned salmon or other staples. They often have a healthier selection than corner stores.
- » Visit the neighborhood farmers' market at the end of the day—farmers will often make some great deals! Many accept EBT.

CHALLENGE I'm not excited to cook just for me or _____.

SOLUTION What solutions can you think of? _____
_____
_____

Cooking for One

▌ What tricks do you know for cooking for one?

Cooking at home can be the easiest way to eat healthy foods consistently. Try to:

» **Plan your meals each week.** Use the same ingredients in many meals but in different ways. For example, buy vegetables that can be eaten both cooked and raw like celery; use in soups, sandwiches, stir-frys and salads.

» **Cook or prep when you have the most energy.** Cut up fruits and vegetables to store, or prep an entire meal. Dinner doesn't have to be the biggest meal of the day, if you have more energy and time in the middle of the day eat your biggest meal then.

» **Eat the most perishable produce first** like lettuce, and save heartier produce like broccoli. Even better—stock up on vegetables like winter squash, onions, and potatoes that last for months outside the fridge.

» **Cook larger batches and freeze.** Cook batches of grains and beans and freeze for easy additions to meals. Soups and casseroles freeze well in single-serving portions.

» **Buy only what you'll eat.** Even if single servings are more expensive at the grocery store, it will still be cheaper than eating out.

» **Keep a stocked pantry.** You'll be more likely to cook if you already have long lasting ingredients like dried goods and seasonings.

» **Buy in bulk.** If you lack storage space, ask a friend to split the bill and the groceries. Choose items that last a long time.

» **Bring extras to a friend or neighbor.** Hopefully, they will return the favor!

▌ Sample Meals

» Eggs are a great single-serving dish. Add veggies, cheese and whole grain toast to make a satisfying meal.

» Start with a dried grain like rice or pasta, add veggies (fresh, frozen or canned), a protein like salmon (fresh, frozen, or canned), and a sauce or flavorings like olive oil and garlic, or soy sauce and ginger.

» Use cooked chicken in a salad with nuts and fruit, or on a sandwich with whole wheat bread.

» Make a Chinese inspired noodle dish: mixed cooked pasta or soaked rice noodles, and stir-fried veggies with a mixture of soy sauce and peanut butter.

» Mix cooked couscous with a dressing of vinegar, olive oil, salt and pepper and lots of fresh veggies, black beans and canned corn.

▌ What's your favorite meal for one?

Saving Time When Cooking

■ **How can you eat well when you're low on time and energy?**

Here are some tips.

» **Learn how to chop vegetables quickly and efficiently.** Most people chop onions slowly. Take a few minutes to learn to do it quickly.

TRY IT! Visit: bit.ly/chop-onion for a chopping demonstration.

» **Pre-chop vegetables** on the weekend or in the morning to cut down on time spent on evening prep. Or, chop more veggies than you need so you are preparing for the next meal. Put them in a reusable containers or plastic bag to store in the refrigerator.

» **Use a sharp knife.** Dull knives are dangerous and require much more energy to use. Also, avoid using a small knife for larger foods.

» **Learn to eyeball common measurements**; know what one cup of chopped veggies looks like on a cutting board or a teaspoon of a spice in the palm of your hand. In most cases, it's not essential to be exact (baking is an exception).

» **Get a head start.** In the morning, lay out any pots or pans you'll need in the evening. If your veggies are already chopped and your pots laid out, you are more likely to cook.

» **Enlist helpers.** Have kids in the house? Ask them to wipe and set the table, wash the veggies, or help gather the ingredients.

» **Try a different tool.** Slow cookers (crock-pots) and rice cookers are great time savers and often available for a few dollars at second-hand stores.

» **Double the yield.** Cook extra chicken one night that can be made into a few different meals like tacos or soup, or used as a salad topper.

» **Keep prepped veggies in the freezer.** Always have frozen vegetables in the freezer—no need to wash or chop!

Small Appliances for Small Spaces

◼ What tricks do you know for using small cooking appliances?

A microwave, pressure cooker, rice cooker, crockpot, or toaster can often be used in place of a larger stove or oven. Search EatFresh.org under the "Limited Kitchen" filter for new recipes!

A **slow cooker, or crock-pot**, is an electric pot that uses very low heat to cook food slowly. (Time: 4-10 hours)
- » has no exposed heat source and does not get hot enough to burn food
- » can be left alone for hours
- » uses less energy than many other appliances
- » inexpensive

Great for: soups, stews, tough meat, dried beans

What would you make in a slow cooker?

A **rice cooker** is an electric pot that uses medium heat to steam food. It works faster than a slow cooker. (Time: 20-60 minutes)
- » shuts off automatically
- » safer than stovetop cooking because it has no exposed heat source
- » inexpensive

Great for: grain or bean dishes, soups, stews, curries, steamed foods

What would you make in a rice cooker?

A **toaster oven** is a very small oven. (Time: same as oven)
- » more energy efficient than a stove for cooking small items
- » great for small spaces

Great for: toasted sandwiches, pizza, fruit crisps, reheating small items

What would you make in a toaster?

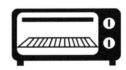

An **electric skillet** works like a skillet on a stovetop. (Time: same as stove)
- » great for small spaces
- » large skillets can be used to cook big items
- » is safer than a hot plate

Great for: eggs, stir-fries, whole-grain pancakes

What would you make in an electric skillet?

A **microwave** cooks food very quickly and is great for small spaces. (Time: a few minutes)

Great for: thawing frozen foods, ready-to-heat foods, hot beverages, steamed rice or vegetables

A few safety tips:
- » Use microwave-safe dishes only. Avoid metal, soft plastic, or Styrofoam!
- » Do not put tightly wrapped or sealed foods in microwave.
- » Poke holes in wrapped items or food skin to vent steam.
- » Rotate and/or stir food a few times during cooking.
- » Be sure to stir liquids after they've been microwaved.

What would you make in a microwave?

© Copyright 2006-2018 Leah's Pantry Food Smarts Workshop • See Instructor Binder for companion info.

Glossary of Recipe Terms

■ Do you know your cooking words?

Connect each term at left to its definition at right.

Food Prep

chop	to rub food on a grater to make shreds
dice	to cut solid food into chunks or medium-sized pieces
grate	to pre-mix food with wet or dry seasonings; helps develop the flavor as well as moisturize it
julienne	to chop into extremely small pieces
knead	to cut solid food into small cubes of the same size
marinate	to cut food into thin strips
mince	to remove the skin of fruits or vegetables
peel	to press dough (i.e. for bread) repeatedly with hands
puree	to beat quickly, in order to add air and volume to food
whip/whisk	to blend until smooth

Cooking

bake	to cook/brown food in a small amount of hot oil
boil	to cook slowly in liquid over low heat, with bubbles barely forming on the surface
broil	to cook with medium heat, usually in an oven
deep fry	to cook with steam, usually in a closed container
fry	to cook over direct heat
grill	to cook in a deep layer of very hot oil
roast	to heat a liquid until the surface bubbles continuously
sauté	to cook in very hot oil
simmer	to cook with medium-high heat, usually in an oven
steam	to cook under strong and direct heat

How to Read a Recipe

What can go wrong if you don't read a recipe well?

It's easy to miss details in a recipe. Perhaps you invent something new...
or have to throw out your dinner!

Smoothies

Prep Time: 5 min   Cook Time: 0 min   Yield: 2 servings

Ingredients:

» 4 frozen strawberries

» 1 cup low-fat plain yogurt

» ½ cup 100% orange juice

» 1 banana, cut into chunks

» 4 ice cubes

Directions:

» Place all ingredients in a blender.

» Cover and process until smooth.

Per Serving: 150 calories, 2g total fat (1g sat),
30g carb, 2g fiber, 65mg sodium

1. Read the recipe well before starting.

   » Make sure you have all the items you need, and enough time for the recipe.

   » Look for any terms you don't know; see page 29 for a guide.

   » When an ingredient is optional, you don't have to use it unless you want to.

   » If necessary, preheat the oven while you prepare.

2. Prepare ingredients for the recipe.

   » If a recipe calls for chopped onion, for example, do the chopping now. You might also need to bring ingredients to room temperature, melt them, or chill them before starting.

   » To learn about ingredient substitutions, check EatFresh.org.

3. Measure carefully.

   » It helps to know abbreviations: **c.** = cup, **T.** or **tbsp**. = tablespoon, **t.** or **tsp**. = teaspoon. It's also helpful to know measurement shortcuts. For example:

      » 4 Tablespoons = ¼ cup

      » 3 teaspoons = 1 Tablespoon

4. Follow the steps in order!

5. If you make any changes to your recipe as you cook, make a note. That way you can prepare the dish exactly the same way next time—or not!

CREATING A BALANCED MEAL

My Plate

What does a balanced diet look like?

Compare your eating pattern with these recommendations from the USDA.

Consume a healthy eating pattern that accounts for all foods and beverages within an appropriate calorie level. **A healthy eating pattern includes:**

» a variety of vegetables—dark green, red and orange, legumes (beans and peas), starchy, and others

» fruits, especially whole fruits

» grains, at least half of which are whole grains

» fat-free or low-fat dairy, including milk, yogurt, cheese, and/or fortified soy beverages

» a variety of protein foods, including seafood, lean meats and poultry, eggs, legumes (beans and peas) and nuts, seeds, and soy products

» minimally processed vegetable oils

A healthy eating pattern limits saturated fats and trans fats, added sugars, and sodium.

» Consume less than 10 percent of calories per day from added sugars.

» Consume less than 10 percent of calories per day from saturated fats.

» Consume less than 2,300 mg per day of sodium.

» If alcohol is consumed, it should be consumed in moderation—up to one drink per day for women and up to two drinks per day for men—and only by adults of legal drinking age.

My Healthy Eating Plate

How does this model, from the Harvard School of Public Health, compare to MyPlate? Why might it be different?

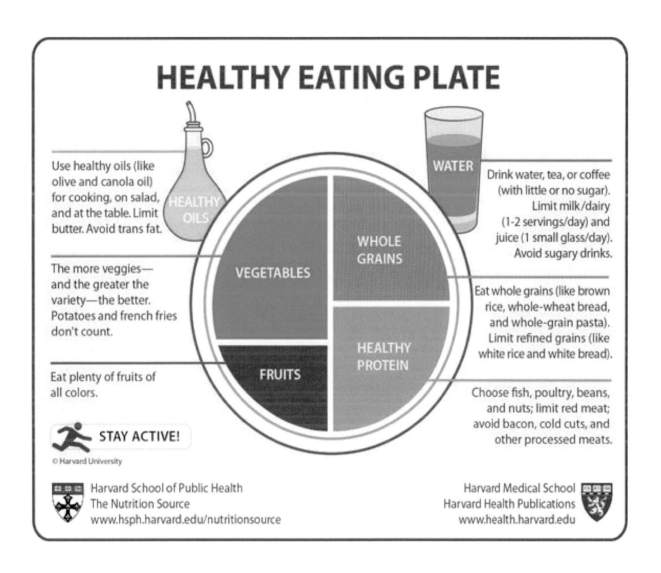

Food Group Bingo

Be the first in your class to complete a row.
Identify an example from each food group.

B	I	N	G	O
Dairy	Protein	Vegetable	Fruit	Grain
Combination	Fruit	Dairy	Protein	Vegetable
Fruit	Grain	FREE	Combination	Protein
Dairy	Protein	Vegetable	Fruit	Grain
Combination	Vegetable	Dairy	Protein	Vegetable

My Family's Rainbow of Fruits and Vegetables

◼ How colorful is your plate?

Fill in the chart with the fruits and vegetables you and your family eat the most. What colors are missing?

Green Foods	Red Foods
Yellow/Orange Foods	**Blue/Purple Foods**
White Foods	**Others**

Eat the Rainbow!

Which color do you eat the most?

Different colored fruits and vegetables are full of nutrients. How can you add variety to your day?

Green Foods

» Lower your chance of getting cancer

» Keep your eyes healthy

» Keep your bones & teeth strong

TRY IT!

spinach	kale
celery	artichokes
green beans	honeydew
broccoli	green grapes
cabbage	green apples
bok choy	limes
cucumbers	avocados
asparagus	

Yellow & Orange Foods

» Keep your heart healthy

» Keep your eyes healthy

» Lower your chance of getting cancer

» Keep you from catching colds

TRY IT!

carrots	cantaloupe
sweet potatoes	tangerines
yellow peppers	mangoes
pumpkins	oranges
pineapple	lemons
papayas	peaches

Red Foods

» Keep your heart healthy

» Keep your bladder healthy

» Keep your memory strong

» Lower your chance of getting cancer

TRY IT!

tomatoes	watermelon
red peppers	red onion
red cabbage	red apples
strawberries	beets
cherries	

Blue & Purple Foods

» Stay healthy when you get old

» Keep your memory strong

» Keep your bladder healthy

» Lower your chance of getting cancer

TRY IT!

eggplant	blueberries
purple cabbage	blackberries
raisins	purple grapes

White Foods

» Keep your heart healthy

» Have good cholesterol levels

» Lower your chance of getting cancer

TRY IT!

onion	ginger
green onion	garlic
cauliflower	jicama
chives	fennel
mushrooms	

36

© Copyright 2006-2018 Leah's Pantry Food Smarts Workshop • See Instructor Binder for companion info.

Know Your Serving Sizes

◼ How big is a serving?

Compare the amounts below. Do you usually eat more, or less?

» **Grains:** 1 slice of bread, 1 tortilla, 1 pancake, ½ cup of cooked pasta or rice

» **Veggies:** 1 medium size piece: 1 tomato, 2 carrots, 1 ear of corn, 9 broccoli florets; 1 cup of leafy greens

» **Fresh fruit:** 1 medium size piece: 1 mango, 1 pear, 2 apricots, 20 grapes, 1 watermelon wedge, 6 canned peach slices

» **Other fruit:** ¼ cup of dried fruit, 6 oz. (¾ cup) 100% fruit or vegetable juice

» **Cheese:** 1.5 oz. (1 index, 1 middle finger)

» **Other dairy:** 8 oz. of milk or yogurt

» **Meat and fish:** 3 oz. (the size of your palm)

» **Snacks:** 1 oz. nuts (1 cupped handful), chips or pretzels (2 cupped handfuls)

» **Processed foods:** make sure to check the label for serving size, since we tend to eat much more than the label states

◼ Tips for Portion Control

» Use smaller plates and cups. Your portion will appear larger than it is.

» Read Nutrition Facts labels to know the serving size and calorie count.

» Order small portions, or serve yourself small portions.

» Share large portions, or put some aside to take home.

» Don't eat straight from the bag.

» Don't eat in front of the TV—it's distracting and has shown to make people eat more!

» Bring healthy snacks with you if you'll be out for long periods—a small bag of nuts, carrot sticks or a piece of fruit are great choices.

Portion Size Hand Comparison

How big is a serving?

Do you usually eat more than these portions, or less?

 Thumb—1 oz. of cheese

 Thumb Tip—1 tablespoon of peanut butter

 Finger Tip—1 teaspoon of butter

 Two Fingers—1½ oz. of cheese

 Palm—3 oz. cooked meat, fish, chicken
1½ pieces of cornbread

 Fist—1 cup cooked pasta, rice, cereal
1 cup cooked beans, peas, lentils
1 cup yogurt, pudding, custard
1 cup salad, 1 baked potato, medium-sized fruit

 Cupped Handful—1 oz. of almonds

 **Two Cupped Handfuls**—1 oz. of chips or pretzels

 Outstretched Hand—2 cups cooked pasta, rice, cereal

CHOOSING WHOLE FOODS

Grocery Store Heroes

Which of these grocery store heroes do you eat often? Which could you add to your diet?

Olive Oil

» **Benefits:** Helps control blood sugar and reduces inflammation.

» **Uses:** Daily! Best for lower-heat cooking. Coat veggies and meat for sautéing or baking. Make salad dressing: mix 3 parts olive oil with 1 part citrus juice or vinegar.

Salmon and Other Cold-Water Fish like Sardines and Mackerel

» **Benefits:** Omega-3 fatty acids can improve insulin sensitivity and reduce inflammation. Also protects against heart disease.

» **Uses:** Bake or broil in the oven with a little olive oil, salt, and pepper. Note that canned fish is an easy, less-expensive option often with similar nutritional benefits to fresh fish.

Spices like Cinnamon, Ginger, Chile

» **Benefits:** Some spices have health-promoting qualities. Cinnamon can help lower cholesterol and blood sugar. Ginger can help with digestion.

» **Uses:** Add to anything for a little extra spice, from baked apples to curry.

Unsalted Nuts and Seeds

» **Benefits:** Healthy fats, vitamins, and minerals that decrease your risk of diabetes and help manage your blood sugar and weight.

» **Uses:** Eat as a snack, top salads or curries, add to yogurt, or play with different nut or seed butters.

Green Veggies like Broccoli, Brussels Sprouts, Kale, Collards

» **Benefits:** Calcium, folic acid, and vitamin K help keep bones strong and protect against heart disease. Full of fiber!

» **Uses:** Steam and drizzle with olive oil or salad dressing. Chop and toss with olive oil and garlic, then sauté or roast at 425° for about 10 minutes or until soft.

Garlic

» **Benefits:** Lowers cholesterol. Helps regulate blood sugar and blood pressure. Supports a strong immune system.

» **Uses:** Add minced, fresh garlic to soups, stews, stir-fries, and sauce. Add powdered garlic (not garlic salt) with butter or oil to mashed potatoes, cooked noodles, or couscous.

Berries

» **Benefits:** Full of antioxidants, lowers risk of heart disease and cancer.

» **Uses:** Eat as a snack, add to yogurt or cereal. Note that frozen berries are an inexpensive, easy way to enjoy berries all year round.

EatFresh.org contains hundreds of recipes using the above ingredients.

© Copyright 2006-2018 Leah's Pantry Food Smarts Workshop • See Instructor Binder for companion info.

Choosing and Using Healthy Fats

■ What are "healthy" fats?

Healthy fats are what your body needs to function properly and they can be found in whole foods such as avocados, fish, nuts, and seeds. Fats and oils are also extracted from whole foods for use in cooking. Some fats and oils are health-promoting, while others are not!

Saturated Fats	Unsaturated Fats		Trans Fats
	Monounsaturated	**Polyunsaturated**	
» come mostly from animals and coconut » are mostly solid at room temperature » can be unhealthy in large amounts » can be unhealthy when very processed or overheated	» come mostly from plants » are very healthy » can be unhealthy when overheated	» come from plants and animals, especially fish » are healthy in limited amounts » can be unhealthy when processed or overheated	» are mostly manufactured from plant oils » act like solid saturated fats in cooking, but are more stable » are unhealthy
Found in: dairy products (butter, cream); fatty meats; coconut products	Found in: peanut products; some nuts and seeds and their oils; avocados; olive oil	Found in: some nuts and seeds and their oils; corn oil; soy oil; some fish	Found in: hydrogenated fats and oils (used in processed foods)

> Even some healthy fats become unhealthy when rancid or overheated. **Smoke point** is the temperature at which a fat or oil begins to burn.
>
> **Remember:** Once a fat or oil starts smoking, it is unhealthy to eat. And never use oil with a bitter taste or odor—it's rancid!

» Use olive oil for salad dressings and low-heat cooking.

» Use butter, coconut oil, or canola oil for medium-heat cooking.

» Use other refined vegetable oils for high-heat cooking; limit total use.

» Avoid hydrogenated fats or lard in cooking.

Eating Out and Staying Healthy

■ **Do you make different food choices when you're away from home?**

It's easy to indulge when eating out. Try these choices.

» Rethink Your Drink: choose water over sugar-sweetened choices.

» Ask for sauces and dressings on the side. Dip instead of pour!

» Choose salsa and mustard over mayo and oil.

» Avoid dishes with these words: au gratin, breaded, buttered, cheesy, creamy, gravy, scalloped, fried, battered.

» Choose dishes with these words: baked, broiled, poached, grilled, roasted, steamed.

» Split entrees with your friend.

» Consider serving sizes carefully. Can your craving for french fries be satisfied by a small instead of a large order?

» If the portions are large, set aside food to take home before you dig in.

» Bring the food home and add a side of raw veggies or fruit to complete the meal.

» Drive by the drive-thru; it's difficult to find healthy fast food on the run!

TRY IT! Try to make a MyPlate meal using this menu. Which items couldn't fit on MyPlate at all?

Starters and Sides $4	**Main Dishes $7**
Sweet Potato Home Fries	*2 Eggs w/Biscuit or Corn Tortillas*
Chips and Guacamole	*Hamburger (add cheese, 50¢)*
Split Pea Soup	*Grilled Cheese with Tomato*
Chicken & Rice Soup	*Mushroom Burger on Whole Wheat Bread*
Small Fruit Salad with Granola	*Tuna Salad Bowl*
Small Garden Salad	*Large Garden Salad with Grilled Chicken*
	Vegetarian Three-Bean Chili

Drinks & Desserts.......................... $3

Small Fresh Orange or Carrot Juice

Milk

Large Soda

Baked Apple

Chocolate Fudge

© Copyright 2006-2018 Leah's Pantry Food Smarts Workshop • See Instructor Binder for companion info.

Eating Foods In-Season

What's growing near you now?

Certain fruits and vegetables grow at certain times of the year. Fresh fruits and vegetables eaten while in-season taste better and provide more nutritional benefits. For example, a strawberry eaten in the summer will be sweeter and will contain more vitamin C than a strawberry eaten in December. The chart below outlines what fruits and vegetables you will see at your local food pantry and farmers' market during each season.

Available All Year

» Beets
» Cabbage
» Carrots
» Cauliflower
» Mushrooms
» Onions
» Oranges
» Potatoes
» Spinach

Summer

» Berries
» Corn
» Eggplant
» Grapes
» Pears
» Tomatoes
» Watermelon
» Zucchini
» Peaches, plums, apricots, cherries

Fall

» Apples
» Peppers
» Sweet potatoes
» Winter squash

Winter-Spring

» Asparagus
» Hard squashes
» Sweet potatoes
» Turnips and broccoli

Make Half Your Grains Whole

▊ Why choose whole grains?

Consider ways to add fiber-rich whole grains to your meals.

Whole grains are usually darker in color and stronger in flavor than refined grains and flours. Eating whole grains has been shown to lower the risk for diabetes, heart disease, high cholesterol, and high blood pressure.

A whole grain contains the germ, endosperm and bran, while a processed grain only contains the endosperm. The germ and bran are the most nutrient rich parts of the grain, and the highest in fiber. Check the ingredient list to make sure you're getting a truly whole grain product: the first ingredient should be something like "whole wheat" and not just "wheat."

REFINED GRAIN FOODS (endosperm only)	WHOLE GRAINS (bran + endosperm + germ)	
» White pasta	» Oats	» Farro
» White bread	» Brown rice	» Spelt
» Most cakes, cookies, and pastries	» Whole wheat	» Quinoa
	» Barley	» Millet
	» Buckwheat	» Teff

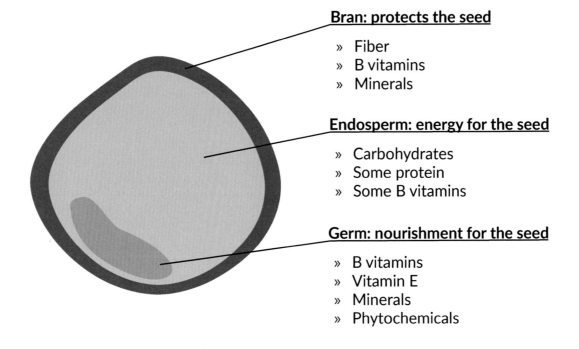

Bran: protects the seed
- » Fiber
- » B vitamins
- » Minerals

Endosperm: energy for the seed
- » Carbohydrates
- » Some protein
- » Some B vitamins

Germ: nourishment for the seed
- » B vitamins
- » Vitamin E
- » Minerals
- » Phytochemicals

DID YOU KNOW? A diet rich in fiber, as found in whole grains and beans, aids digestion and keeps you full for longer. Make sure to get 3 servings of whole grains and 4½ cups of fruits and veggies each day for the recommended amount of fiber.

◼ How much sugar is in your favorite drink?

» Use the nutrition facts to find out.
» Check the number of servings per container. Will you drink more than one?
» For each serving, do the math: grams of sugar ÷ 4 = teaspoons of sugar
  For example: 40g sugar ÷ 4 = 10 teaspoons sugar

TRY IT! Now do the math on these other soft drinks. How many teaspoons of sugar in each serving? In each bottle or can?

ORANGE SODA
Nutrition Facts

Serving Size 8 oz.
Servings per Container 2

Amount per Serving

Calories 168 Calories from Fat 0

Total Fat 0g
    Saturated Fat 0g
    Trans Fat 0g
Cholesterol 0mg
Sodium 50mg
Total Carbohydrate 42g
    Dietary Fiber 0g
    Sugars 42g
Protein 0g

Vitamin D 0% Calcium 0%
Potassium 0% Iron 0%

CHOCOLATE MILK
Nutrition Facts

Serving Size 8 oz.
Servings per Container 1

Amount per Serving

Calories 193 Calories from Fat 81

Total Fat 9g
    Saturated Fat 5g
    Trans Fat 0g
Cholesterol 35mg
Sodium 125mg
Total Carbohydrate 20g
    Dietary Fiber 0g
    Sugars 20g
Protein 8g

Vitamin D 15% Calcium 25%
Potassium 10% Iron 0%

CHOCOLATE MILK

SWEET TEA

SWEET TEA
Nutrition Facts

Serving Size 8 oz.
Servings per Container 3

Amount per Serving

Calories 144 Calories from Fat 0

Total Fat 0g
    Saturated Fat 0g
    Trans Fat 0g
Cholesterol 0mg
Sodium 50mg
Total Carbohydrate 36g
    Dietary Fiber 0g
    Sugars 36g
Protein 0g

Vitamin D 0% Calcium 0%
Potassium 0% Iron 0%

COLA
Nutrition Facts

Serving Size 1 can (12 fl. oz.)
Servings per Container 1

Amount per Serving

Calories 150 Calories from Fat 0

Total Fat 0g
    Saturated Fat 0g
    Trans Fat 0g
Cholesterol 0mg
Sodium 50mg
Total Carbohydrate 40g
    Dietary Fiber 0g
    Sugars 40g
Protein 0g

Vitamin A 0% Vitamin C 0%
Iron 0% Iron 0% Calcium 0%

ORANGE SODA

COLA

[content continues on next page...]

Drink water instead!

» Add lemon to your water for extra flavor. Or try the recipe below.

» Experiment with hot, cold, and room temperature water to see what you like best.

» Have a glass of water on the table at every meal, and nearby when working.

» Drink a glass in the morning after waking up.

» Drink water instead of snacking.

» Drink water when you eat out. It's free!

» Note that in many places, tap water is held to higher purity standards than bottled water! Bottled water also sits in plastic. This may be harmful to human health and the earth. Consider saving money and going green—drink local tap water from a reusable glass or metal bottle.

Flavored Water Recipe

Fill a pitcher with cool water.

Add ½ cup thinly sliced cucumber and ½ cup fresh mint leaves. Chill in refrigerator. Enjoy!

Try different combinations of flavors:

» Thin slices: lemon, lime, orange, grapefruit, cucumber, apple, berries, melon, pineapple, fresh ginger

» Fresh whole leaves or sprigs: mint, basil, rosemary, parsley

Make These Meals Healthier

■ **How would you make the following meals healthier?**

Use the guidelines of MyPlate or the Healthy Eating Plate to help. Include more vegetables, whole grains, legumes, fruits and dairy... and use your imagination!

Meal 1	Meal 2	Meal 3	Meal 4	Meal 5
Fried chicken White rice Salad with lettuce and cucumbers Whole milk	Hamburger on white bun French fries Milk shake	Pasta Tomato sauce Garlic bread with butter Soda	Instant Ramen Chips Juice	Stir-fry with beef and white rice

Go, Slow, STOP!

 Which foods are healthy to eat every day?

Which are best to avoid? To help decide, we can group foods by the colors of the stoplight.

» A Go food is a fresh, whole food. We want to eat mostly Go foods.

» A Slow food is minimally processed, and can often be a healthy choice.

» A STOP! food is a highly processed food that we should avoid eating.

What examples would you add to each group?

⬤ Go!

» Corn on the cob

» Brown Rice

» An Orange

» Milk

More examples: _____

⬤ Slow

» Canned corn

» White rice

» Orange juice

» Yogurt

More examples: _____

⬤ STOP!

» Corn Flakes (or another generic cereal made from corn)

» Rice Cereal Treats

» Orange soda

» American cheese slices

More examples: _____

Grain Game

Can you identify different whole grains?

Whole grains are a nutritious, filling alternative to refined grain foods such as white pasta. Experiment by using them in soups or as salad bases, breakfast cereals, or side dishes.

__ AMARANTH: Combine 1 cup amaranth with 2½ cups of water in a pot and bring to a boil. Cover and simmer for 20 minutes, until water is absorbed. Amaranth can also be popped like popcorn in a skillet.

__ BARLEY: Add 1 cup of barley to 3 cups of boiling water, cover and cook for 45 minutes or until barley is tender and water is absorbed. Choose whole barley instead of pearled for more nutrients.

__ BUCKWHEAT (or kasha): Place 1 cup of buckwheat in a pot and cover with 2 cups of water. Cover and boil for 15-20 minutes, or until all the water is absorbed. Buckwheat is gluten-free.

__ BULGUR WHEAT: The finer ground the bulgur, the shorter time it needs to be cooked. For a medium grind, pour 2½ cups of boiling water over 1 cup of bulgur. Cover and let stand for 30 minutes, or until the water is absorbed. Bulgur wheat is a great option for a limited kitchen.

__ COUSCOUS: Bring 1½ cups of water to a boil in saucepan, take off the heat, add 1 ½ cups of couscous, cover and let sit for 5-10 minutes, then fluff with a fork. Couscous is a great option for a limited kitchen. Choose whole wheat couscous for more nutrients.

__ MILLET: Add 1 cup millet to 2½ cups water in a saucepan. Bring to a boil, cover and simmer for 25 minutes. Make it creamier by adding more water and stirring frequently while cooking.

__ OATS: Cook 1 cup of oats in 2 cups of water. For rolled oats, cook 15 minutes and for steel-cut oats, cook for 30 minutes.

__ QUINOA: Bring 1½ cups of water to a boil and add 1 cup of rinsed quinoa. Cover and cook for 15 minutes. Quinoa is gluten-free.

__ WHEAT BERRIES: Bring 3 cups of water to a boil and add 1 cup of wheat berries. Simmer uncovered for 45 minutes and drain before serving.

__ BROWN RICE: Boil 2 cups water and add 1 cup rice. Cover and cook for about 45 minutes.

Bean Game

■ What beans do you know?

Beans are a great source of protein and fiber, and have been shown to lower cholesterol and blood pressure, reduce risk of certain cancers, and aide with digestion. Rinse and pick through your beans before soaking or cooking to discard any discolored beans. Do not use salt or any acidic ingredients until the beans are finished cooking, otherwise the beans might not soften. Use beans in soups, salads, burritos or tacos, or mash them to make a dip.

__ SOY BEANS: Used to make soy milk, tofu, and tempeh. Soak for 8 hours or overnight. The water will rise while cooking soybeans, so make sure that the dried beans only come up to one fourth of the height of the pot, and the water should come up to one third of the height of the pot. Cook for 3 hours.

__ GARBANZO BEANS (or chickpeas): Used to make hummus and falafel, in addition to being a great addition to soups and salads. Soak overnight, then drain and cover with twice the amount of water than beans. Cover and cook for 1 hour.

__ BLACK BEANS: Soak overnight, then drain and cover with 3 cups of water for each cup of beans. Cook for 45 minutes to 1 hour.

__ GREEN SPLIT PEAS: There is no need to soak split peas, just bring to a boil 1 cup of peas with 3 cups of water and simmer for 30-45 minutes.

__ RED "CHILI" BEANS: Soak overnight, drain and cover 1 cup of beans with 2 cups of fresh water. Boil for 1½ -2 hours.

__ LENTILS: A quick and versatile ingredient full of healthy protein. There are many different varieties, but they can all be cooked the same way. There is no need to soak lentils, simply simmer 1 cup of lentils with 2 cups of water for 20-45 minutes, depending on their size.

__ KIDNEY BEANS: Soak overnight, drain the water, and cover 1 cup of beans with 3 cups water. Cook for 1-1½ hours.

__ BLACK-EYED PEAS (or "cow-peas"): Often used in Southern cooking. No need to soak black-eyed peas, just cover 1 cup of the black-eyed peas with 3 cups of water in a big pan and boil for 45 minutes to 1 hour.

__ PINTO and __NAVY BEANS: Soak overnight, drain the water and cover 1 cup of beans with 3 cups of water. Cook for 1-1½ hours.

Don't Call Me Sugar!

**There are many names for the sugar added to food.
Can you find the ones hidden here?**

BARLEY MALT

BROWN SUGAR

CANE JUICE

CORN SYRUP

DEXTRIN

DEXTROSE

FRUCTOSE

GLUCOSE

HONEY

LACTOSE

MALTOSE

MAPLE SYRUP

MOLASSES

SWEETENER

```
H  O  N  E  Y  F  E  M  A  T  R  A  P  S  A
M  E  N  U  K  S  W  E  E  T  E  N  E  R  N
T  A  N  I  R  A  H  C  C  A  S  E  H  F  A
U  R  R  S  O  R  B  I  T  O  L  O  M  R  Y
R  N  I  R  T  X  E  D  C  R  A  C  A  U  W
G  A  S  M  M  E  E  O  J  I  S  L  P  C  T
L  I  G  R  B  A  R  L  E  Y  M  A  L  T  E
U  E  T  U  Y  N  M  X  Q  O  E  C  E  O  E
C  S  E  S  S  A  L  O  M  S  E  T  S  S  W
O  U  L  Y  L  N  K  L  O  T  L  O  Y  E  S
S  O  R  T  H  Y  W  R  E  T  C  S  R  B  A
E  U  O  D  H  T  T  O  O  N  L  E  U  H  R
P  S  T  P  G  X  V  Z  R  T  U  P  P  F  T
E  T  C  M  E  W  B  C  A  B  D  M  G  A  U
S  T  R  D  B  C  A  N  E  J  U  I  C  E  N
```

BONUS Can you find these artificial sweeteners too?
These are chemicals with few or no calories.

ASPARTAME   NUTRASWEET   SACCHARIN   SORBITOL

The Leah's Pantry DO EAT Food List

■ **What are your "go-to" healthy foods?**

Check the list below. Do you see any of your favorites?

Whole Grains & Other Complex Carbohydrates

Some carbohydrates are "complex." They take a lot of work for your body to break down. These provide more nutrients and help you feel full longer.

Examples: brown rice, whole wheat products (bread, tortillas), oatmeal, quinoa, amaranth, lentils, beans, starchy fruits and vegetables

Healthy Fats

The human body needs different kinds of fats for health. Without fat, the body cannot use some vitamins. Children's brains need healthy fats too. Fats are also slow to digest. This can help you stay full for a long time. Choose fats in their natural state.

Examples: avocados, whole nuts and nut butters (low-salt or unsalted), peanuts and peanut butter, olives and olive oil, seeds, fatty fish like salmon and sardines

Colorful Vegetables

Different colored vegetables and fruits have different nutrients. To get a variety, try to "eat the rainbow" every day. Enjoy them raw and cooked different ways, too. Enjoy leafy greens as often as possible.

Whole Fruits

Whole, fresh fruits contain natural sugars in small amounts. These sugars give quick energy. They also come packaged with vitamins, minerals, and fiber. Choose colorful fruits. Enjoy them raw or minimally cooked.

Protein from Plants

Whether you're a vegetarian or not, enjoy some protein from plants. These foods often have more fiber and less saturated fat than animal products. They can also be cheaper and last longer.

Examples: beans, lentils, nuts and nut butters, seeds and seed butters, tofu and tempeh

Healthy Beverages

The healthiest drinks have no added sugars. They are made with clean water and/or only whole, natural ingredients. They can be flavored with fruits, herbs, spices or vanilla extract.

Examples: water flavored with fresh fruit, herbal teas, unsweetened milk and milk substitutes (i.e. almond, soy)

 **Can you make a SMART Goal about adding one of these foods to your diet? For recipe ideas, check** EatFresh.org.

Healthy Swaps

True or False: Healthy foods always cost more money than unhealthy foods?

Changing to healthier foods doesn't necessarily mean spending more money.

Instead of...	Try...	Cost
potato chips	popcorn	$0.85 vs. $0.45 per serving
white rice	brown rice	5 lb. bags are equal in price; bulk is much less than boxed
white pasta	whole wheat pasta	sometimes same price
white flour tortillas	corn, or whole wheat tortillas	corn is cheapest; white and whole wheat are comparable
white potatoes	sweet potatoes	white potatoes are less expensive, but with MUCH less nutrition
sugary "kids" cereal	oatmeal with honey and dried fruit	$4 a box vs. 42 oz. for $1.99
white bread	whole wheat or whole grain	white bread is less expensive, but has no nutritional value

BEING A SMART CONSUMER

▎ What do you look for on a nutrition label?

There's a lot of information to read; try choosing one or two items to concentrate on at a time.

① Check the Serving Size and Servings per Container. Remember the nutrition facts label is for one serving. Your package might have more than one serving. If you are eating two servings, then you need to double everything on the labels.

② Calories tells you how much energy you get from eating one serving of this food. Fat-free does not mean calories-free. Items that are fat-free, low-fat, or reduced-fat might have the same amount of calories as the full fat version.

③ The total fat on the label might include monounsaturated and polyunsaturated fats, which are "good fats" that can help lower blood cholesterol. "Zero Trans Fat" foods don't always mean the food is trans-fat-free. The law allows a small amount of trans fat per serving in foods. Read the ingredient list and look for "partially hydrogenated oils" to see if the food has trans fat. Consume foods low in added sugars, saturated fats, and sodium. Cut back on foods higher in these nutrients.

④ Getting enough dietary fiber, vitamins, and minerals can improve overall health and help reduce the risk of some diseases. Choose foods with higher % Daily Value for these nutrients. Fiber also promotes healthy bowel function.

⑤ The footnote states that the % Daily Value on the nutrition label is based on a 2,000-calorie-diet. This is a recommendation. The amount that each person needs depends on their caloric needs. It also breaks down the nutrient needs for a 2,500 calorie eating pattern.

⑥ % Daily Value on the nutrition labels helps you determine if a serving of that specific food is high or low in those nutrients. The guide is to choose products that are 5% Daily Value or less for things you want to limit like saturated fat, and sodium. Look for 20% Daily Value or more for things you want to eat more of.

[content continues on next page...]

① Start here

② Check calories

③ Limit these nutrients

④ Get enough of these nutrients

⑤ Footnote

⑥ Quick guide to % DV

5% or less is Low

20% or more is High

Nutrition Facts

2 servings per container
Serving Size 1 cup

Amount Per Serving

Calories 250

	% Daily Value
Total Fat 12g	18%
Saturated Fat 3g	15%
Trans Fat 3g	
Cholesterol 30mg	10%
Sodium 470mg	20%
Total Carbohydrate 31g	10%
Dietary Fiber	0%
Sugars 5g	
Protein 5g	
Vitamin D	4%
Calcium	2%
Iron	20%
Potassium	4%

* The % Daily Value (DV) tells you how much a nutrient in a serving contributes to a daily diet. 2,000 calories a day is used for general nutrition advice

(Adapted from pre-2015 USDA labels style)

Food Labels—Ingredients Lists

■ Have you ever seen a strange item on an ingredients list?

Some of these are just new names for ingredients you already know. But others may be chemicals or allergens you don't want. Mark any ingredients below that you'd like to avoid.

- ❑ **Whole grain** (such as whole wheat or oats) still has all its original nutrients, including fiber and vitamins. Whole grains can keep you full for longer than refined grain products like white flour.

- ❑ **Food dyes** can be natural or artificial. Several food dyes have been banned in the United States. Others, such as Blue #1, Blue #2, Red #40, and Yellow #6, are banned in other countries but are still available in the US.

- ❑ **Hydrogenated** fats and oils are used to extend the shelf life of baked goods. However, these are harmful trans fats. They can increase your heart disease risk.

- ❑ **Fructose** is a type of natural sugar found in fruits and some vegetables. ❑ **High fructose corn syrup** is a sweetener made by concentrating the fructose from corn. Manufacturers use it—especially in soft drinks—because it is cheaper and sweeter than white sugar. But because the sugar in high fructose corn syrup is so concentrated, it's easy to eat too much.

- ❑ **Sucrose** is the same as white table sugar.

- ❑ **Monosodium glutamate (MSG)** is a flavor enhancer. It is used to "stretch" meaty flavors in cheap, processed foods without much natural taste. ❑ **Yeast extract** and ❑ **hydrolyzed proteins** are used the same way.

- ❑ **Aspartame, saccharin, acesulfame,** and **sucralose** are artificial sweeteners with few or no calories. These are controversial because they may increase your appetite for sweet foods. ❑ **Stevia** is a low-calorie sweetener from the stevia plant.

- ❑ **Natural flavors** do not add nutrients to food. They may come from any natural source, even strange ones like tree bark or bugs!

- ❑ **Citric acid** comes from citrus fruits. It is used to give foods a sour flavor or as a natural preservative.

Food Labels—Ingredients Lists (CONTINUED)

These vitamins and minerals are added to processed foods to make them more nutritious:

- ❑ Niacin or niacinamide
- ❑ Thiamin
- ❑ Riboflavin
- ❑ Vitamin A palmitate
- ❑ Zinc oxide
- ❑ Pyridoxine
- ❑ Folic acid
- ❑ Iodized salt (table salt with iodine added)
- ❑ Calcium carbonate

Your best bet when shopping: Choose foods with a short list of ingredients you recognize!

TRY IT! Match the ingredient labels below with the products shown on page 58 by writing the corresponding number in each circle.

INGREDIENTS:
Whole Grain Oats, Sugar, Oat Bran, Corn Starch, Honey, Brown Sugar Syrup, Salt, Tripotassium Phosphate, Canola Oil, Natural Almond Flavor. Vitamin E (mixed tocopherols) added to preserve freshness.

Answer: Honey oat cereal (number four)

INGREDIENTS:
Carbonated Water, Sugar, Orange Juice from Concentrate (3.7%), Citrus Fruit from Concentrate (1.3%), Citric Acid, Vegetable Extracts (Carrot, Pumpkin), Sweeteners (Acesulfame K, Sucralose), Preservative (Potassium Sorbate), Malic Acid, Acidity Regulator (Sodium Citrate), Stabilizer (Guar Gum), Natural Orange Flavorings with Other Natural Flavorings, Antioxidant (Ascorbic Acid).

Answer: Orange soda (number two)

INGREDIENTS:
Enriched Corn Meal (Corn Meal, Ferrous Sulfate, Niacin, Thiamin Mononitrate, Riboflavin, and Folic Acid), Vegetable Oil (Corn, Canola, and/or Sunflower Oil), Flamin' Hot Seasoning (Maltodextrin [Made From Corn], Salt, Sugar, Monosodium Glutamate, Yeast Extract, Citric Acid, Artificial Color [Red 40 Lake, Yellow 6 Lake, Yellow 6, Yellow 5], Sunflower Oil, Cheddar Cheese [Milk, Cheese Cultures, Salt, Enzymes], Onion Powder, Whey, Whey Protein Concentrate, Garlic Powder, Natural Flavor, Buttermilk, Sodium Diacetate, Disodium Inosinate, and Disodium Guanylate), and Salt.

Answer: Spicy hot corn chips (number one)

INGREDIENTS:
Corn Syrup, Sugar, Palm Oil, and Less Than 2% of Mono- and Diglycerides, Hydrogenated Cottonseed Oil, Malic Acid, Salt, Soy Lecithin, Artificial Flavors, Blue 1, Red 40, Yellow 5.

Answer: Taffy candy (number three)

Food Label Scavenger Hunt

◼ What do you look for on a food label?

Look at two labels for similar products.

» **Goal:** Learn how to read the food label and pick the product that is better for your body.

» **Instruction:** The facilitator will pass out two nutrition labels. Complete the questions below by comparing the two nutrition labels, then circle Label A or B.

Which food label has...

1. More **calories** per serving	Label A	Label B
2. More **sugar** per serving	Label A	Label B
3. Less **sodium** per serving	Label A	Label B
4. More **saturated fat** per serving	Label A	Label B
5. More **fiber** per serving	Label A	Label B
6. More **calories** from fat	Label A	Label B
7. More **protein** per serving	Label A	Label B
8. More **total fat** per serving	Label A	Label B
9. More **calcium** per serving	Label A	Label B
10. Which is the **healthier** choice?	Label A	Label B

Food Advertisements

Where do you see food advertisements?
How do these influence people's choices?

Think about the different ways ads try to reach people. Consider the ad below.

» Who is the sponsor of this ad?

» What techniques are used to sell this product?

» Who is the target audience?

» What is the message of this ad?

» What useful information does this ad provide? Does it give any misleading information?

Creating a Food Advertisement

» Work in groups of three to develop a persuasive food ad. You may use a recipe from class, or any other food you like.

» Draw the ad on the paper (map it out on scrap paper first). Use both words and pictures. Use the six questions above to help plan your ad.

» Present your ad to the class.

Nutrition Labels Comparison

▮ Can you guess what kind of product these labels come from?

Pick two of these labels to use with the Food Label Scavenger Hunt activity.

Nutrition Facts

Serving Size 1 bar

Servings per Container 8

Amount Per Serving

Calories 90	Calories from Fat 23

	% Daily Value*
Total Fat 2.5g	4%
Saturated Fat 0.5g	3%
Trans Fat 0g	
Cholesterol 0mg	0%
Sodium 50mg	2%
Total Carbohydrate 15g	5%
Dietary Fiber 1g	4%
Sugars 6g	
Protein 2g	
Vitamin A	1%
Vitamin C	0%
Calcium	0%
Iron	2%

* Percent Daily Values are based on a 2,000 calorie diet. Your daily values may be higher or lower depending on your calorie needs.

		Calories:	2,000	2,500
Total Fat	Less than		65g	80g
Sat Fat	Less than		20g	25g
Cholesterol	Less than		300mg	300mg
Sodium	Less than		2400mg	2400mg
Total Carbohydrate			300g	375g
Dietary Fiber			25g	30g

Ingredients: granola (rolled oats, tapioca syrup, sugar, sunflower oil, sea salt, vanilla extract, baking soda), Tapioca Syrup, Crisp Rice (rice flour, sugar, raisin juice concentrate, sea salt, annatto color), Semisweet Chocolate Chips (sugar, chocolate liquor, cocoa butter, dextrose, soy lecithin, vanilla), Dry Roasted Peanuts, Peanut Butter Chips (sugar, cocoa butter, partially defatted peanut flour, sea salt, cocoa, soy lecithin), Rice Flour, Glycerin, Whole Oat Flour, Sunflower Oil, Peanut Butter (peanuts, salt), Molasses

Nutrition Facts

Serving Size 1 bar

Servings per Container 6

Amount Per Serving

Calories 100	Calories from Fat 23

	% Daily Value*
Total Fat 2.5g	4%
Saturated Fat 1.5g	3%
Trans Fat 0g	
Cholesterol 0mg	0%
Sodium 60mg	2%
Total Carbohydrate 18g	6%
Dietary Fiber 1g	4%
Sugars 7g	
Protein 1g	
Vitamin A	0%
Vitamin C	0%
Calcium	2%
Iron	5%

* Percent Daily Values are based on a 2,000 calorie diet. Your daily values may be higher or lower depending on your calorie needs.

		Calories:	2,000	2,500
Total Fat	Less than		65g	80g
Sat Fat	Less than		20g	25g
Cholesterol	Less than		300mg	300mg
Sodium	Less than		2400mg	2400mg
Total Carbohydrate			300g	375g
Dietary Fiber			25g	30g

Ingredients: rolled oats, rice flour, corn syrup, sugar, fructose, coconut, palm oil, contains 2% or less of dextrose, molasses, glycerin, salt, sorbitol, natural flavor, malt extract, butter, soy lecithin, nonfat milk, mixed tocopherols, rosemary extract (for freshness), wheat starch

*Nutrition Labels, Original Style
(Pre-2015 Dietary Guidelines)*

Nutrition Facts

8 Servings per Container

Serving Size   1 bar

Amount Per Serving
Calories   120

	% Daily Value*
Total Fat 3g	5%
Saturated Fat 1g	3%
Trans Fat 0g	
Cholesterol 0mg	0%
Sodium 110mg	5%
Total Carbohydrate 24g	8%
Dietary Fiber 3g	10%
Total Sugars 11g	
Includes 9g Added Sugars	
Protein 2g	
Vitamin D 0mcg	0%
Calcium 48mcg	4%
Iron 3mg	11%
Potassium 329mg	7%

* The % Daily Value (DV) tells you how much a nutrient in a serving of food contributes to a daily diet. 2,000 calories a day is used for general nutrition advice.

Ingredients: whole grain oats, enriched flour (wheat flour, niacin, reduced iron, thiamin mononitrate, riboflavin, folic acid), whole wheat flour, vegetable oil (high oleic soybean and/or canola oil), soluble corn fiber, sugar, dextrose, fructose, calcium carbonate, whey, wheat bran, cellulose, potassium bicarbonate, natural and artificial flavor, mono- and diglycerides, soy lecithin, wheat gluten, niacinimide, vitamin A palmitate, carrageenan, zinc oxide, guar gum, pyridoxine hydrochloride, thiamin hydrochloride; filling: invert sugar, corn syrup, glycerin, apple puree concentrate, sugar, blueberry puree concentrate, natural and artificial flavors, raspberry puree concentrate, modified cornstarch, sodium alginate, citric acid, malic acid, methylcellulose, dicalcium phosphate, red 40, blue 1

Nutrition Facts

12 Servings per Container

Serving Size   1 bar

Amount Per Serving
Calories   144

	% Daily Value*
Total Fat 5g	6%
Saturated Fat 0g	2%
Trans Fat 0g	
Cholesterol 0mg	0%
Sodium 83mg	3%
Total Carbohydrate 23g	7%
Dietary Fiber 2g	8%
Total Sugars 8g	
Includes 6g Added Sugars	
Protein 3g	
Vitamin D 0mcg	0%
Calcium 18mcg	1%
Iron 1mg	5%
Potassium 97mg	2%

* The % Daily Value (DV) tells you how much a nutrient in a serving of food contributes to a daily diet. 2,000 calories a day is used for general nutrition advice.

Ingredients: whole grain oats, almonds, raisins, honey, canola oil, cinnamon, salt

Nutrition Labels, New Style
(2015 Dietary Guidelines)

Outsmarting the Grocery Store

▊ Do you know?

» Where are the healthiest foods are located?

» Are products displayed at the ends of aisles always on sale?

» Is there usually a difference in price between name brand and generic products? What about quality?

» Why are candy and magazines always near the register?

» Where are the most expensive products located on the shelves? What about cereals marketed to kids?

» When should you put refrigerated and frozen foods in your basket? Why?

▊ A few tips:

» Unit prices allow you to compare the price of two packages that may contain a different amount of food.

32 OZ LF YOGURT	
UNIT PRICE	RETAIL PRICE
$0.05 per oz	$1.62
84651972554813	

6 OZ LF YOGURT	
UNIT PRICE	RETAIL PRICE
$0.12 per oz	$0.72
8465197846659	

» Larger packages often have lower unit prices; however, be sure to consider whether you'll be able to eat the entire amount before it goes bad. Find stores that carry bulk foods.

» Generic products are often identical to name brand products in everything but price.

Anatomy of a Grocery Store

■ **How does the layout of your grocery store shape your choices?**

Draw a diagram that shows what you would find in each part of the store.

Creating a Meal Plan & Grocery List

▌ What would you like to cook this week?

Planning your meals ahead of time saves time, saves money, and encourages heathier eating. It's also a great way to teach your kids about the "real world," so get them involved!

▌ How do I do it?

» Plan your meals for the week. Be sure to include some recipes you will make.

» Using the recipes, make a grocery list that includes all of the ingredients for each recipe. Make sure to check your kitchen for staples such as olive oil, salt and pepper. You probably don't need to buy everything.

» Sort your grocery list according to type of food: produce, meat, dairy and dry goods.

» Grocery shop! Save the receipt to help create a budget for the future.

» Review your receipt afterwards. Do you see anything surprising? Save the receipt to help create a budget for the future.

▌ Meal Plan & Grocery List Sample

Meals	Grocery list	
E.g. Hearty Egg Burritos (*eatfresh.org/recipe/main-dish/hearty-egg-burritos*)	Produce	*1 head garlic* *1 bunch green onion* *1 bell pepper-green or red*
	Meat	
	Dairy	*Eggs* *Low-fat cheddar cheese*
	Dry, Canned, or Boxed	*1 package whole wheat tortillas* *Canola Oil* *1 can black beans*

[content continues on next page...]

TRY IT! Now try making your own plan and list.

THIS WEEK'S meals	SHOPPING list
	Produce
	Meat
	Dairy
	Dry/Canned/Boxes
	Other

Meal Plan & Grocery List Follow-Up

Now discuss the planning activity.

What meal(s) did you plan to make last week?

Did you follow through with your meal plan?

Did you face any challenges in following through with your plan?
If so, what were they?

What meals would you like to prepare for this week?

Seafood and Mercury

▌ What can make seafood harmful to eat?

Nearly all fishes have traces of mercury, the same heavy metal found in old-fashioned thermometers.

Mercury occurs naturally in the environment and can also be found in the air released from industrial pollution. When mercury falls from the air, it accumulates in streams and oceans and is turned into methylmercury in the water. Fish and shellfish that live in this environment absorb the methylmercury and retain it. Some types of fish and shellfish have higher mercury than others, depending on what the fish eat, the species of fish, the age and size, and the type of water in which it is found.

Generally, fish-eating fish have higher levels than herbivorous or smaller fish. Within the same species of fish, older and larger fish have higher levels of methylmercury than smaller fish.

For most people, there is no health risk from the mercury in fish and shellfish. The health risk from mercury depends on the amount eaten and the levels of mercury inside the fish and shellfish. Thus, the Food and Drug Administration (FDA) advise women who may become pregnant, pregnant women, nursing mothers, and young children to avoid certain types of fish and shellfish and instead eat the ones that have lower mercury levels.

TRY IT! To learn what seafood is safest in your area, visit seafoodwatch.org.

▉ Have you visited a Farmers' Market?

These can be a great way to stock up on fresh, local, and affordable produce each week. If your neighborhood has a farmers' market, consider making this part of your weekly routine.

Get the most for your money by...

»   Buying produce that is in season and abundant. Look to see which veggies and fruits are well-stocked. (See p. 35.)

»   Shopping near the end of the market hours. Farmers don't want to leave with produce and are often willing to give deals instead of bring food back with them.

»   Deciding how you will use the produce you purchase before you buy it to avoid waste.

    »   Are these veggies or fruit good eaten raw?

    »   Do I know how to prepare this food?

    »   Do I have resources/recipes to cook if the ingredients are unfamiliar?

Good questions to ask (or have your kids ask) the farmers:

»   "I notice your produce is not certified organic. What are your growing practices? Do you spray or use chemical fertilizers, pesticides, or fertilizers?"

»   "I notice your produce is certified organic. How do you control for pests and weeds? What are the hardest items to grow organic?"

»   "How do you suggest I prepare this food? I'm looking for some new ideas."

»   "Are there any new items we can expect in the next few weeks?"

»   "Do you grown your own produce or get it from other farmers?"

TRY IT!   Go to EatFresh.org to find farmers' markets near you.

Do You Qualify for a Nutrition Assistance Program?

» For: eligible low-income people and their families

» You are not eligible if you receive SSI, but Social Security Retirement Benefits are okay

» Even if you receive SSI, other members of your household may be eligible

» All legal residents are eligible

» Call 1-877-847-3663 or visit calfresh.gov

» Use CalFresh to buy fresh fruits and vegetables, whole grains, lean proteins, and more

» Each month, CalFresh benefits are issued on an electronic benefit transfer (EBT) card—like an ATM card

» The EBT card can be used at most grocery stores, discount stores, farmers' markets and neighborhood stores

» Restaurant Meals: if you are 60 or older, disabled, or homeless you may be eligible to purchase prepared meals at certified restaurants

» Nutrition for Women, Infants and Children

» For eligible low-income pregnant or breastfeeding women, new moms, and children under 5

» 1-888-942-9675 or wicworks.ca.gov

Other Programs

» School Nutrition Programs

   » For: eligible low-income school-aged children

   » Contact your local school

» TEFAP—The Emergency Food Assistance Program

   » For: eligible low-income persons

   » Visit fns.usda.gov/tefap/eligibility-and-how-apply

TRY IT! Visit mybenefitscalwin.org for applications and more information.

SF·MARIN
FOOD BANK

Code dates on products do not mean that food is unfit for consumption!
Please refer to these handy guidelines for code date extensions.

Shelf-Stable Foods Extensions

Product		Storage Life Past Code Date
Staples		
Beans, Dried (pinto, red, black, etc)		12 months
Canned Goods Low Acid (meats, beans, corn, soup, etc.)		5 years
High Acid (pineapple, tomatoes, pickles, etc.)		18 months
Cereal (hot and cold varieties)		12 months
Coffee, (and Decaf)	Ground in Cans	2 years
	Instant	12 months
Egg Noodles, Dry		2 years
Flour	White	12 months
	Whole Wheat	1 month
Pasta, Dry (spaghetti, macaroni, penne, etc.)		2 years
Rice	Brown Rice	12 months
	White or Wild	2 years
Sugar	Brown, Raw	4 months
	White, Granulated	2 years
Beverages		
Bottled Water (all varieties)		12 months
Capri Sun		2 months
Cocoa, Cocoa Mixes		indefinitely
Crystal Light		2 months
IZZE Sparkling Beverage		12 months
Juice Boxes		6 months
Powdered Drink Mix		6 months
Sodas	Diet (cans or bottles)	3 months
	Regular (cans or bottles)	9 months
Tetrapak: Soy Milk, Almond Milk, Rice Milk, or Coconut Milk		1 month
Condiments & Snacks		
Beef Jerky		12 months
Chocolate Syrup		2 years
Condiments (bbq sauce, jam/jelly, ketchup, mayo, mustard, salsa, salad dressing, syrup, olive/vegetable oil)		12 months
Cookies, Packaged		2 months
Crackers (Saltines, *Ritz, Triscuits*, etc.)		8 months
Evaporated Milk		12 months
Extracts		4-5 years
Granola Bars (*Nutrigrain, Nature Valley*, etc.)		12 months
Microwave Popcorn		18 months
Peanut Butter		9 months
Popcorn (dry kernels)		2 years
Slim Jims		18 months
Spices	Fresh Spices	5-7 days
	Ground or Dried Spices	2-3 years
	Whole Spices	3-4 years
Vegetable Oil Spray		2 years
Vinegar		2 years

This information is to be used as a guide only. It was developed based on general knowledge, industry practices, and the understanding that best before dates are about sensory quality. All information taken from the Food Marketing Institute www.fightbac.org, EatByDate LLC www.eatbydate.com, Food Banks Canada www.foodbanksbc.com, and Feeding America "Donor Requirements & Restrictions"

[content continues on next page...]

Bakery Items

Product		Shelf Storage Past Code Date	Refrigerator Storage Past Code Date	Freezer Storage Past Code Date
Bagels		1 day	7 days	2 months
Bread	Sliced	4 days	14 days	3 months
	French, loaf, etc	1 day	14 days	2 months
Cakes	Angel food	2 days	7 days	2 months
	Chiffon, sponge	2 days	7 days	2 months
	Chocolate (unfrosted)	2 days	7 days	4 months
	Pound cake	4 days	7 days	6 months
Cookies		3 weeks	2 months	10 months
Croissants		1 day	7 days	2 months
Danish		2 days	7 days	2 months
Muffins		2 days	7 days	2 months

Refrigerated Foods Extensions

Product		Storage Life Past Code Date
Beverages		
Juices		
	Citrus juices, pasteurized (orange, grapefruit, etc.)	7 days
	Odwalla, Naked Juice (100% juice and smoothies)	consume by code date
	Punches, juice blends	14 days
Tetrapak: Soy Milk, Almond Milk, or Rice Milk		7-10 days
Dairy Products		
Butter		1-3 months
Cheeses	Hard cheese (cheddar, swiss, etc.)	6 months
	Shredded Cheese (parmesan, mozzarella, etc.)	1 month
	Cottage Cheese	21 days
	Cream Cheese	60 days
Dips (sour cream based)		14 days
Eggs (whole)		5 weeks
EggBeaters (egg substitute)		60 days
Margarine		1-3 months
Milk (all varieties)		7 days
Sour Cream		21 days
Whipping Cream/Aerosol Whipped Cream		30 days
Yogurt		10 days
Deli Products		
Fruit, cut		consume by code date
Hot Dogs, Lunch Meats (bologna, Ham, etc.)		consume/freeze by code date
Lunchables		consume/freeze by code date
Pesto		consume/freeze by code date
Salsa		consume by code date
Dough Products		
Cookie Dough		consume/freeze by code date
Pasta (fresh)		2 days
Pie Crust (ready-to-bake)		consume/freeze by code date
Tube Cans (biscuits, rolls, pizza dough, etc.)		consume by code date
Soy Products		
Dips (soy/tofu based)		7 days
Soy Milk		7 days
Tofu (all varieties)		21 days

SAVING MONEY: TIPS TO STORE YOUR PRODUCE TO MAKE IT LAST LONGER

1. KEEP YOUR PRODUCE WHOLE

Don't even rip the stem out of an apple until you eat it. As soon as you start pulling fruits and vegetables apart you've broken cells and given a surface for microorganisms to grow. Mold proliferates rapidly and contaminates everything nearby, so toss any spoiled produce immediately.

2. KEEP INCOMPATIBLE FRUITS AND VEGGIES SEPARATE

You might have heard that to speed-ripen a peach, you put it in a closed paper bag with a ripe banana. Some fruits (like bananas) give off high levels of ethylene – an odorless, colorless gas – that speeds up ripening of nearby ethylene-sensitive produce. "Gas releasers" are one of the main causes of premature decay. One bad apple really can spoil the whole bunch. Use our quick reference guide to the right and keep all "gas releasers" (the first two groups) separate from ethylene-sensitive produce (the third group.)

3. KNOW WHAT TO REFRIGERATE AND WHAT TO LEAVE OUT

The main way to lengthen shelf life of produce is by using cold temperatures to slow food's respiration, or 'breathing' process, so less ethylene gas is emitted and the ripening process is slowed. The warmer the temperature, the faster the rate of respiration, which is why refrigeration is critical for most produce. But while you want to slow it down, you don't want to stop the breathing altogether. The worst thing to do is seal fruits and vegetables in an airtight bag, because you'll suffocate them and speed up decay.

A big part of correct storage is knowing what to refrigerate. Cold-sensitive fruits and veggies lose flavor and moisture at low temperatures. Store them on the counter, not in the fridge. Once they're fully ripe, you can refrigerate them to help them last, but for best flavor, return them to room temp. Never refrigerate potatoes, onions, winter squash or garlic. Keep them in a cool, dry, dark place, and they can last up to a month or more. Light and heat will cause them to sprout. But separate them so their flavors and smells don't migrate.

New innovations: Some products you can purchase absorb ethylene and can be dropped into a crisper with vegetables. A variety of produce bags both absorb ethylene and create an atmosphere that inhibits respiration.

QUICK STORAGE TIPS:

REFRIGERATE THESE "GAS RELEASERS":
- Apples
- Apricots
- Canteloupe
- Figs
- Honeydew

DON'T REFRIGERATE THESE "GAS RELEASERS":
- Avocados
- Bananas, unripe
- Nectarines
- Peaches
- Pears
- Plums
- Tomatoes

STORE THESE AWAY FROM ALL "GAS RELEASERS":
- Bananas, ripe
- Broccoli
- Brussels sprouts
- Cabbage
- Carrots
- Cauliflower
- Cucumbers
- Eggplant
- Lettuce and other leafy greens
- Parsley
- Peas
- Peppers
- Squash
- Sweet potatoes
- Watermelon

[content continues on next page...]

4. KNOW WHAT TO EAT FIRST

Eat more perishable items first and save the longer-lasting produce for later in the week. Use this quick guide to help you decide what to eat first. The timing suggestions are for ready-to-eat produce, so allow extra days for ripening if you're buying not-quite-ripe fruits or vegetables.

5. STORAGE STARTS WITH THE SHOPPING BAG

Many people don't realize storage starts even before the shopping bag makes it home. Shop for less perishable items like potatoes, onions, and melons first and keep heavier items on the bottom of the bag. Shop for more perishable items berries and broccoli last so they don't get warm while you shop (and emit more ethylene gas, which will ripen them faster). Get the produce home quickly and into dark cool place or into your refrigerator if you have one. The earlier you shop at the farmers market the fresher the produce will be, the less time it has spent outside in warm temperatures, and the longer it will last at home.

6. HAVE A BACKUP PLAN

If you find yourself with more ripe produce than you can eat, have a strategy for how to use it up quickly. Our favorite for the cool San Francisco weather is using a crock pot to make an easy potful of soup with any leftover vegetables. Get creative and try a new recipe, like a big pie for your neighbor or a pot of tomato sauce to freeze in individual packages.

Some fruits and vegetables can be strored in the freezer for using later. Fruits like berries are fine to freeze as-is. Fruits that tend to brown easily, like apples or peaches, should be soaked in an acidic juice before freezing to help them maintain their color.

Most vegetables need to be blanched before freezing, which involves submerging them briefly in boiling water or steaming to destroy the enzymes that cause spoiling. Onions, peppers, and herbs do not need to be blanched. Squash, sweet potatoes, and pumpkin should be fully cooked before freezing. All other vegetables should be blanched.

To blanch by boiling, use at least a gallon of water for a pound of vegetables. Put the vegetables in a wire basket, submerge them completely in the boiling water, cover with a lid, and begin timing. To blanch by steaming, put the vegetables in a steamer basket and suspend it above an inch or two of boiling water. Cover the pot, and begin timing as soon as steam starts to escape from under the lid. With either method, shake the basket a couple of times to ensure that all vegetable surfaces are exposed to the heat. After the allotted time, remove the basket, and plunge the vegetables into a bowl of ice water to stop the cooking. Once cool, remove them, drain thoroughly, and package for freezing. Package all produce tightly to avoid freezer burn.

The amount of time you should leave each variety of vegetable submerged in boiling water varies. Use the internet or a library book to look up specific instructions.

TIME IT RIGHT:
EAT FIRST (WITHIN 1–3 DAYS):
- Artichokes
- Asparagus
- Avocados
- Bananas
- Basil
- Broccoli
- Cherries
- Corn
- Dill
- Green beans
- Mushrooms
- Mustard greens
- Strawberries
- Watercress

EAT SECOND (WITHIN 4–6 DAYS):
- Arugula
- Cucumbers
- Eggplant
- Grapes
- Lettuce
- Lime
- Zucchini

EAT THIRD (WITHIN 6–8 DAYS):
- Apricots
- Bell peppers
- Blueberries
- Brussels sprouts
- Cauliflower
- Grapefruit
- Leeks
- Lemons
- Mint
- Oranges
- Oregano
- Parsley
- Peaches
- Pears
- Plums
- Spinach
- Tomatoes
- Watermelon

EAT LAST (LONGEST LASTING):
- Apples
- Beets
- Cabbage
- Carrots
- Celery
- Garlic
- Onions
- Potatoes
- Winter squash

A big thank you to *Vegetarian Times* for the valuable information.

STAY HEALTHY

Fuel Your Brain

◼ How can eating whole foods help your brain?

Breakfast

Maintaining energy and concentration is an essential part of a healthy lifestyle. Breakfast is the first place to start. A good breakfast may help you keep steady energy and moods later in the day.

Choose to eat a healthy, balanced breakfast over sugar and caffeine.

Instead of...	Try...
sugary cereal	oats or shredded wheat
coffee	green tea
juice	whole fruit or diluted juice
pastries, danishes, or donuts	whole wheat toast w/cream cheese or peanut butter
skipping breakfast	eating breakfast!

Lunch

What do you eat for lunch? Do you bring it from home or get it at school? How do you feel before lunch—hungry or famished? How do you feel after lunch—energized or sleepy?

Choose to eat a healthy, balanced lunch (and a mid-morning snack).

Instead of...	Try...
potato chips	almonds or sunflower seeds
soda	water or milk
candy	fruit
pizza or fast food	veggie wrap or turkey sandwich

Make Moving Fun!

What are your favorite ways to move?

Kids need 60 minutes of exercise daily. Adults need 150 minutes of moderate activity per week or 75 minutes of vigorous activity per week.

» Limit "Screen" Time (TV, video games, mobile devices, computers); the number of hours of TV children watch per week is directly correlated with obesity. Children who watch more than three hours of television a day are 50% more likely to become obese than children who watch fewer than two hours.

» Physical activity affects more than just weight. It can also improve mood, sleep, and concentration!

» If you have a tough time getting motivated, look for ways to be active with others—find a class, go for walks or dance with a buddy, add physical games to a family party.

"The easiest way to reduce inactivity is to turn off the TV. Almost anything else uses more energy than watching TV."
  - Dr. William H. Deitz

THINK ABOUT IT

Do you get enough exercise every week? Does your family?

What are some ways to move more during your day?

Getting Exercise in Small Spaces

» Jump rope
» Jumping jacks
» Dance parties
» Wrestling
» Housework
» Stairs instead of the elevator
» Yoga or stretching
» Hula hoops

 **How can you create a SMART Goal to achieve the changes suggested here?**

Healthy Changes

1 Carla, a 65 year old woman, often complains about being tired. Her doctor is also concerned she is at risk for diabetes due to her weight, family history, ethnic background, and moderately high blood pressure. When Carla wakes up, she always has coffee but sometimes doesn't eat more than a slice of white bread with butter. For lunch, she eats from the cafeteria at work and snacks during the day on fruit, chips, candy and diet soda. If she has food in the house, she has a reasonably sized dinner that includes a simple salad, pasta, chicken and rice, or hamburgers. Otherwise she's often too tired to go to the grocery store after work and eats frozen pizzas, cereal, or whatever she can find. She has never exercised regularly and isn't sure what she should do to start.

2 Laura is a single mother of 3 children who works full time. In the morning, she hurries to get the kids ready for school and daycare. She rarely has time to eat before going to work, and never has time to pack a lunch. She doesn't feel hungry until the afternoon but drinks a lot of coffee and diet soda at work. By the evening, she hardly has any energy to make dinner and help the kids with their homework. They eat a lot of frozen fish sticks and junk food. In order to occupy the kids while she makes dinner, they watch TV. Even though she hardly eats all day, she's still not able to lose much of the weight she gained after her last baby.

3 Jesse hates to get up in the morning! She would rather sleep in than eat breakfast. But by the time she gets to school, she feels hungry and tired. She often falls asleep in class. She eats mostly from the school cafeteria, but usually chooses foods like chips, juice, and french fries. After school, she often snacks on soda, cookies, and candy. Her mom always comes home and cooks a healthy dinner.

4 Tony is an athlete who has practice almost every day after school. He needs to eat a lot! He eats cereal in the morning, lunch in the cafeteria and a fast food meal every day before practice. His mom makes big dinners like fried chicken and mashed potatoes. Although he's really active, Tony is worried he weighs too much—but he's also concerned about having enough energy to play.

5 Jill doesn't eat regular meals. If she's up in time, she eats breakfast but often skips lunch because she doesn't like the food in the cafeteria. She drinks a lot of diet soda but eats mostly fruit, cheese, veggies, and bread. She stays up late at night and often eats around 11pm. Her family doesn't eat dinner together usually because everyone has a different schedule.

» What changes would you suggest to these individuals and/or their caregivers?

» What will be the hardest changes for them to make?

» Can you think of a SMART Goal each one could try to achieve?

Sleep Your Way to Health

Do you get enough rest?

Sleep is important for mental health and weight control. If you answer yes to any of these questions, you may be sleep deprived!

» Crave caffeine to get going in the morning, and junk food later in the day?

» Fall asleep within five minutes of laying down?

» Gain weight and don't know why?

» Have memory trouble?

» Want to take a nap right now?

Fill in the Blanks

1. You may eat _____ when you're tired.

2. Most adults need at least 7–9 _____ of sleep per night, even seniors. Children need more.

3. Your brain can _____ itself during sleep by getting rid of waste.

4. Sleep helps the brain form _____.

5. During deep sleep your _____ pressure drops. Breathing slows and blood flow moves to the muscles.

6. The Challenger shuttle disaster and Chernobyl nuclear accident have been blamed on errors related to _____ deprivation.

7. It should take about 10–15 _____ to fall asleep. If you always fall asleep faster, you may be sleep deprived.

8. _____ are the only mammal that delay sleep on purpose.

9. While you're asleep, your _____ switches from cleansing your body to rebuilding it.

10. Growth _____, which help the body grow and heal, are released during sleep.

Word bank:

hours

liver

minutes

more

humans

memories

sleep

blood

hormones

clean

Diabetes: Know the Risk

▎Do you know your diabetes risk?

Family background may play a role in your risk for diabetes. But lifestyle makes a difference, too.

Risks

You have higher risk for Type 2 diabetes if you:

» are overweight

» are over 45 years old

» have had a parent, brother, or sister with diabetes

» have family background that is Alaska Native, American Indian, African American, Hispanic/Latino, Asian American, or Pacific Islander

» have had gestational diabetes or given birth to a baby weighing more than 9 pounds

» have had abnormal cholesterol levels

» exercise less than 3 times per week

» have polycystic ovary syndrome (PCOS)

» on previous testing, had impaired fasting glucose or glucose tolerance

» have history of cardiovascular disease

Symptoms

Nearly 6 million Americans have Type 2 diabetes and do not know it. Some show no signs or symptoms. Others do not know what to look for:

» increased hunger and/or thirst

» fatigue

» increased urination, especially at night

» weight loss

» blurred vision

» sores that do not heal

Diabetes is a disease in which the body does not produce enough insulin. As a result, the body cannot use sugar well. Type 1 diabetes usually appears in childhood or young adulthood. It cannot be prevented. Type 2 diabetes can develop at any age. It can be prevented or delayed through healthy lifestyle.

Fortunately, you can reduce your risk!

» Reach and maintain a reasonable body weight.

» Make wise food choices most of the time.

» Be physically active every day.

» Lower your intake of sodium and alcohol.

» Talk with your doctor about whether you need medication to control your blood pressure or lower your cholesterol levels.

 **TRY IT!** **How can you create a SMART Goal to achieve the changes suggested here?**

Sodium and Healthy Blood Pressure

◼ Do you or a family member have high blood pressure?

A desirable blood pressure is 120/80. Your blood pressure is high at 140/90 and above. Have your blood pressure checked at least once a year. High blood pressure means your body is working harder than it should to move blood to all parts of your body.

High blood pressure raises your risk of...

» stroke

» heart attack

» kidney problems

» eye problems

» death

High blood pressure can be preventable

» Stay active.

» Reduce sodium intake.

» Reduce alcohol intake.

» Maintain a healthy weight.

◼ Test your Sodium Smarts!

You've heard a lot about limiting sodium from foods, but what else should you know? Answer True or False to the questions below. (Here's a clue: only one item is false!)

		True	False
1.	Healthy individuals should keep intake under 2300 mg a day; those with high blood pressure or high risk should keep intake to under 1500 mg a day.		
2.	Whole fruits and vegetables do not contain sodium.		
3.	Soy sauce, canned foods, and seafood can be high-sodium foods.		
4.	Potassium helps to balance the sodium in your body; therefore, eating plenty of high-potassium fruits and vegetables may help maintain healthy blood pressure.		
5.	A food with less than 140 mg of sodium per serving can be labelled a "low-sodium food."		

 **TRY IT!** How can you create a SMART Goal to achieve the changes suggested here?

How can you keep your bones strong?

Bones can become fragile as we age. Bone loss cannot be reversed, but it can be prevented or delayed. Treatment and care include intake of calcium and Vitamin D, weight bearing exercise, prevention of falls, and bone-friendly medicines. Eat plenty of calcium-rich foods (see chart) to ensure you are getting enough calcium to build and maintain strong bones.

Getting Enough Calcium Through Foods

» Adults 19-50 years old should get 1,000 mg of calcium each day. Adults over 50 years of age should get 1,200 mg each day.

» Eat 3 to 4 servings of dairy or enough of other high calcium foods each day. (See chart below.)

» Read Food Labels: 100% of the Daily Value (%DV) = 1000 mg. Add a zero to the end of the percentage to get milligrams (mg) of calcium in one serving. (Example: 30% DV equals 300 mg of calcium.)

No Dairy? No Problem!

These foods are also high in calcium: sardines, tofu made with calcium sulfate, orange juice with calcium, calcium-fortified bread, salmon, spinach, turnip greens, cooked or raw kale, raw Chinese cabbage, broccoli, cauliflower, and calcium-fortified products.

Food	Calcium	% Daily Value
yogurt, 8 oz.	415 mg	42%
skim/whole milk, 8 oz.	300 mg	30%
cheddar cheese, 1 oz.	306 mg	30%
frozen yogurt, ½ c.	103 mg	10%
ice cream, ½ c.	85 mg	9%

 **DID YOU KNOW?** Weight-bearing exercise like weight lifting can increase muscle mass and protect your bones as you age.

Made in the USA
San Bernardino, CA
16 August 2019